NATIONAL GEOGRAPHIC

Climbing to Success

PATHFINDER EDITION

By Jacqueline St. Jacques

CONTENTS

CLIMBING TO SUCCESS

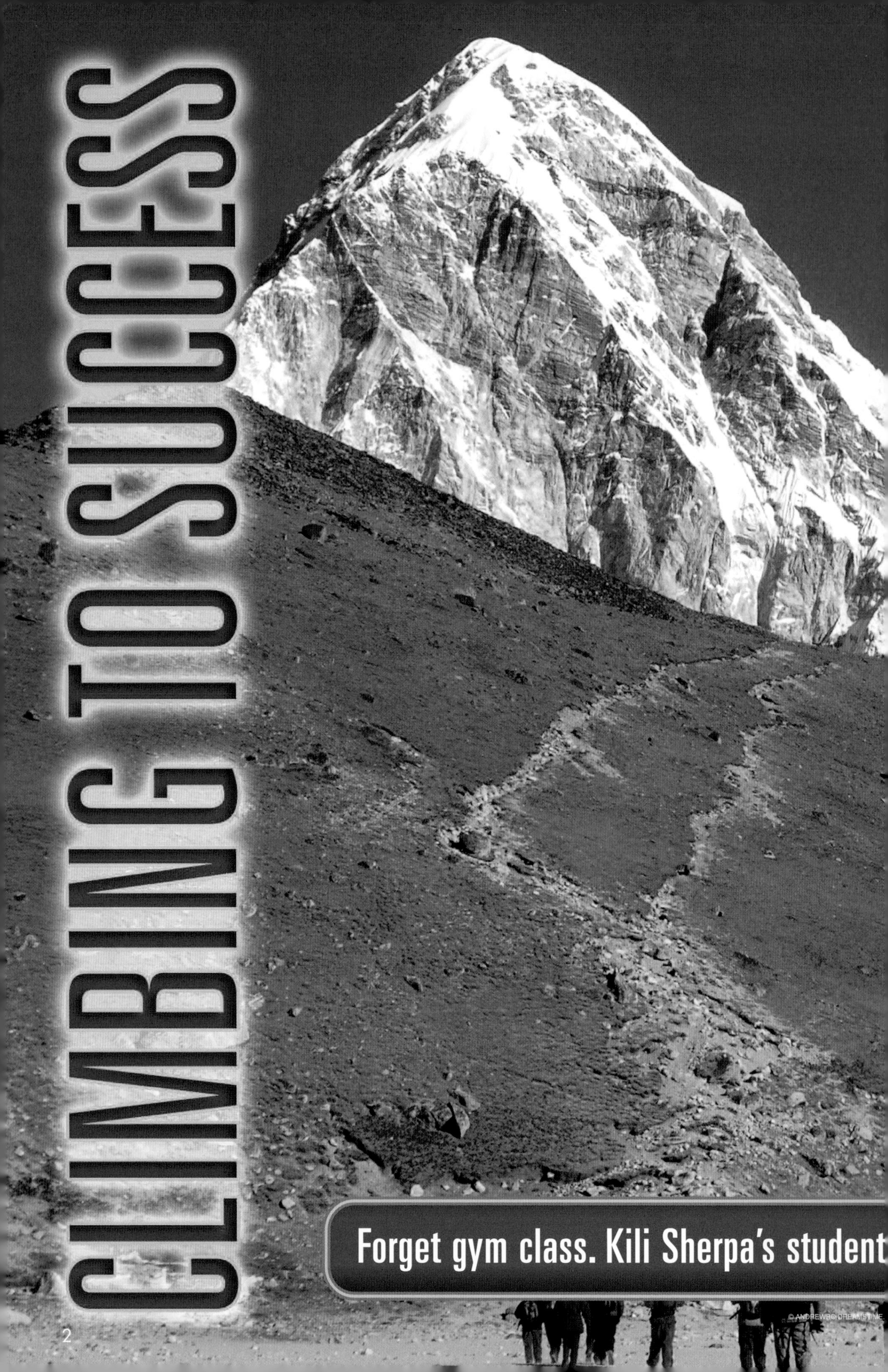

© ANDREWBO/DREAMSTIME

Forget gym class. Kili Sherpa's student

Peak Experience. ***After decades of helping others climb Everest, Nepal's Sherpa people started launching their own expeditions in 1991.***

earn how to climb—and survive—Earth's tallest mountains.

BY JACQUELINE ST. JACQUES

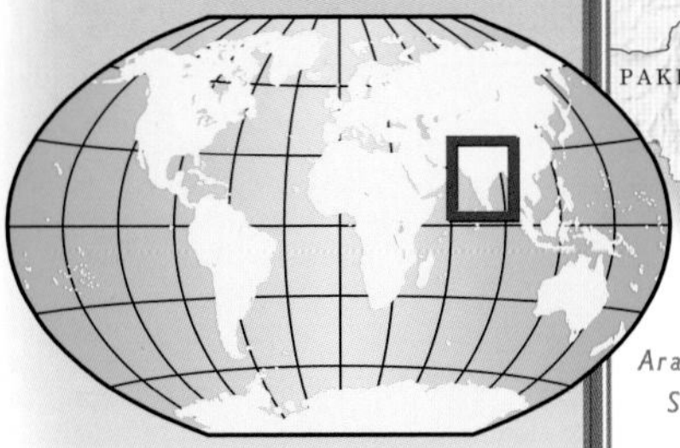

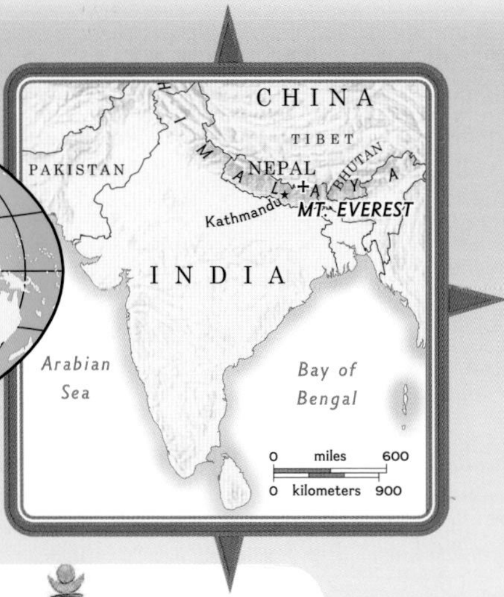

Kili Sherpa always knew what he'd be when he grew up—a mountain climber. He wanted to **scale,** or climb, the Himalaya. These peaks tower over Kili's village in the Asian country of Nepal.

The tallest peak of all is Mount Everest. It rises 29,028 feet above sea level. That's the highest point on the entire planet.

Some of Kili's relatives worked on expeditions, or trips, in the Himalaya. They carried gear and helped climbers. Kili loved hearing their stories. And he eagerly practiced climbing the 100-foot rock near his house.

Sure enough, Kili became a skilled climber and guide. He made it to the summit, or top, of Everest in 2000. But Kili now has another job too. It's one he never expected.

Kili Sherpa is a teacher.

Hometown Hero. ***Kili Sherpa (in purple) leads kids through his village.***

The Sherpas' Story

Kili's life may sound unusual. How many professional climbers do you know? But working in the mountains is common for Kili's people—the Sherpas.

Sherpas are a group of roughly 25,000 people. Their ancestors lived in Tibet, which is now a part of China. The name "Sherpa" is Tibetan for "eastern people."

In the early 1500s, many Sherpas **migrated,** or moved, to Nepal. They built villages, grew potatoes and other crops, and raised shaggy beasts called **yaks.** Despite the move, though, Sherpas clung to their language and traditions.

Looking around their new home, Sherpas could hardly miss the incredible Himalaya. Indeed they honored the mountains as homes of their gods. The one thing Sherpas didn't do was *climb* the mountains. That came later.

Big Business

"Later" was the early 1900s. That's when Alexander Kellas, a British explorer, hired Sherpas to carry equipment for his expeditions. The Sherpas' strength and bravery amazed him. So did their ability to work hard without complaining.

In no time, Sherpas became the backbone of Everest exploration. In fact, a Sherpa named Tenzing Norgay was the first person photographed atop Mount Everest. He and Edmund Hillary, a beekeeper from New Zealand, were the first people to reach Everest's summit. They did so on May 29, 1953.

After that, Everest expeditions grew into big business. Like Kili, half the Sherpa population now works in the mountaineering world. They set up campsites, take care of equipment, and cook. Sherpas also do the hard, risky work of marking the route up the mountain.

Dangerous Jobs

Kili and other skilled climbers earn far more than they could by farming or trading. But they may also face grave dangers.

The "mountain without mercy," as one writer called it, has killed more than 150 people.

Mountaineers have died in storms and **avalanches.** They've also gotten sick from being so high above sea level. All too many Sherpas know climbers who never came home.

No one can make the Himalaya safe. Kili Sherpa realizes that. But he also knows how learning the right skills can help climbers survive. He got concerned when he saw young, untrained Sherpas being hired for dangerous jobs.

"Someone should teach them," he thought.

Learning the Ropes. ***Kili Sherpa (in cap) keeps a firm grip on a student's climbing rope (below). That helps students scale the rock safely (right).***

Wordwise

avalanche: large amount of snow, ice, rock, or dirt that slides down a mountain

crampons: metal spikes attached to climbers' boots to help them grip the ice

migrate: to move from one place to another

scale: to climb

yak: Asian animal related to the cow

Skill + Sense = Safety

Kili Sherpa opened the Solu-Khumbu Sherpa Climbing School in 1996. Each spring and fall, children, teens, and young adults come to learn the basics of climbing. Lessons are free.

"Safety comes first," Kili tells students. "Always check your knots and remember to look after your equipment." Ropes need special care, he emphasizes.

That's because climbers often wear metal spikes, called **crampons,** on their boots. Crampons are great for gripping the ice. But they can also slash ropes. So climbers must step carefully.

Kili also offers tips for being a smart climber. "Never panic," he says. "Remember that the rope has you. Always feel the rock with your hands and feet for holds. Often your eyes will not detect the holds. Keep three points [a combination of hands and feet] on the rock at all times."

Practice Makes Possible

Kili teaches students how to put on a climbing harness and tie knots. Then he drills them in key techniques. These include

- **belaying:** holding ropes so that another climber can move up safely,
- **jumaring:** using rope-gripping tools to climb up, and
- **rappelling:** sliding down a rope.

Students practice these moves over and over. "When you are at high altitudes," Kili says, "the skills must be automatic."

Peak Opportunities

Students spend days climbing and learning with Kili. The training, he realizes, is just part of a Sherpa's education. Yet it "allows the basic skills to become second nature to them before they move on."

After studying with Kili, students can begin doing simple jobs on expedition teams. As they work and watch, they'll learn even more. "It often takes years," he notes, "before someone may make their first important climb."

Kili's first students are already climbing to new opportunities. Some have even worked on Everest expeditions. Kili hopes the next generation of Sherpas will reach great heights.

And then, he really hopes, they'll come back down.

Physical Education. ***Kili Sherpa's students learn to climb by tackling large rocks.***

The Seven Summits

"The Seven Summits" is the name given to the highest mountain on each continent. Look at the map and chart below to see how these peaks compare.

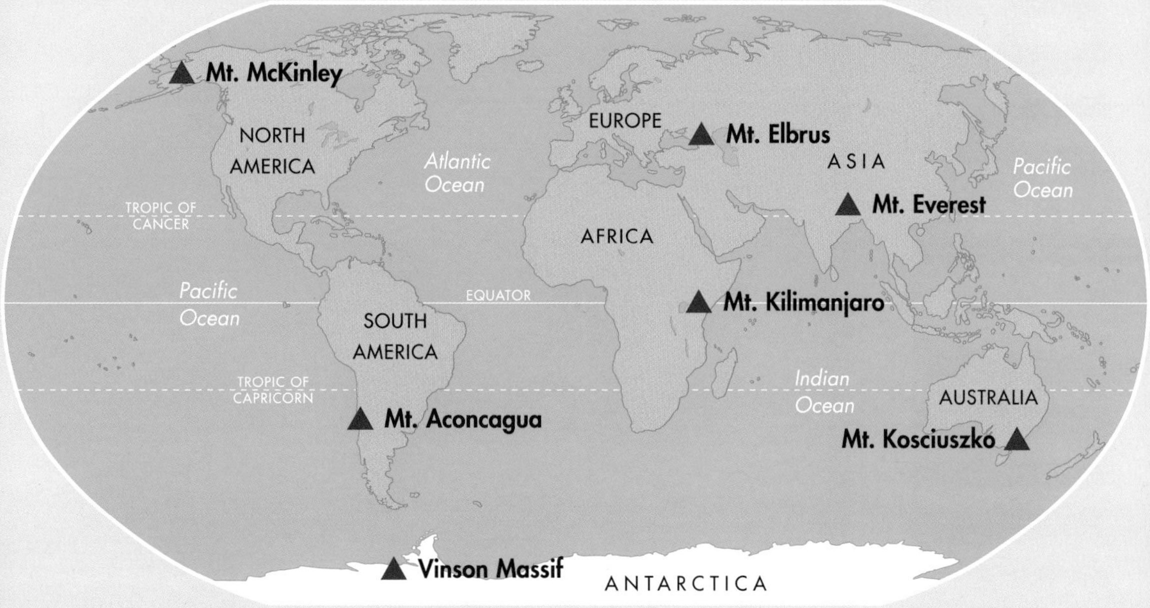

Mountain	Continent	Elevation	First Climbed
Mount Aconcagua	South America	22,834 feet	1897
Mount Elbrus	Europe	18,510 feet	1874
Mount Everest	Asia	29,028 feet	1953
Mount Kilimanjaro	Africa	19,340 feet	1889
Mount Kosciuszko	Australia	7,310 feet	1840
Mount McKinley	North America	20,320 feet	1913
Vinson Massif	Antarctica	16,067 feet	1966

Scaling Mount Everest

ICE AX: ***tool swung into walls of ice, allowing climbers to hold on***

CARABINER: ***metal link that connects climbing rope to piton***

PITON: ***metal spike driven into rocky cracks to serve as an anchor for ropes***

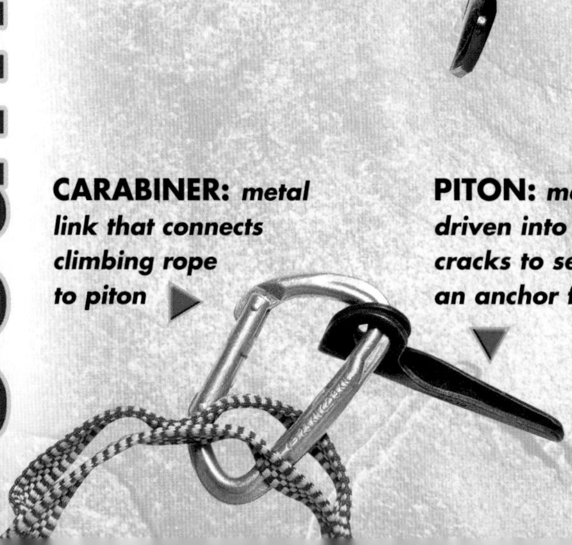

Making It to the Top

Everest towers above climbers' tents (left). To reach the peak, the climbers rely on these tools of the trade (below).

ICE SCREW: ***large metal screw twisted into ice to create an anchor for ropes***

CAM: ***device that opens inside a crack, providing an anchor for ropes***

CRAMPONS: ***metal spikes that help climbers' boots grip the ice***

The Race

A Peak Experience. ***Tenzing Norgay raises a flag at the peak of Mount Everest. He and Edmund Hillary were the first people ever to reach this summit.***

For many years, people thought reaching the summit of Mount Everest was impossible. Yet that didn't stop them from trying. Mount Everest was the ultimate challenge. To reach its summit meant making history. They wanted to be the first to conquer the world's tallest mountain.

Climbing to New Heights

In the early 1950s, many men looked for fame on Mount Everest. The mountain couldn't be climbed alone. So the men formed climbing teams. The members of a team worked together to scale Everest. Yet each man dreamed of being the first to the top.

To reach the summit, climbers needed skill and experience. They needed courage. They also needed a little luck. A British climbing team had just that in May 1953.

On May 26, two climbers from the team trekked up the mountain. They got within 300 feet of the peak. Then they had a problem with their gear. Disappointed, they had to turn back.

Edmund Hillary and Tenzing Norgay were next to try. They left their camp at 6:30 a.m. on May 29. They slowly made their way along a steep slope. Soon they came to a 40-foot-high rocky step. Hillary led the way. The two men wriggled upward through a crack to the top. They crisscrossed along a narrow ridge. Then they did what no one had done before. They hiked up the snow-covered dome to the summit. Hillary reached the top at 11:30 a.m. Norgay was just a few feet behind him.

to the Top

Setting Records

The success of Hillary and Norgay inspired people all over the world. Climbers wanted to set new records. They scaled Mount Everest from different sides. They took different routes to its summit.

These people had something in common. They were all men. No woman had ever reached the mountain's peak. A Japanese woman named Junko Tabei changed that.

Tabei was a music teacher, journalist, and mother. She started climbing when she was ten years old. Tabei was only 4 feet 9 inches tall. Yet she was a world-class mountain climber.

In May 1975, Tabei led the first all-female expedition to the top of Everest. The women were experienced climbers. Yet Tabei almost didn't make it. An avalanche buried her in snow. Luckily, someone spotted her boots sticking out of the snow. She was rescued. Tabei was badly bruised and her glasses were broken. But she pushed forward. Twelve days later she became the first woman to make it to the top of Mount Everest.

Daring to Climb

Today, climbers still trek up Mount Everest. The journey to the peak is dangerous. Yet for many people, making it to the top of the world is worth the risks. Since Hillary and Norgay's famous hike, about 1,600 people have reached Mount Everest's summit. More than 70 were women.

A Female First. ***Junko Tabei celebrates atop Mount Everest in 1975. She was the first female to make it to the summit.***

Mount Everest

Answer these questions to discover what you learned about the world's tallest mountain.

1. Where is Mount Everest located?
2. When did Sherpas begin to climb Mount Everest? Why?
3. Why did Kili Sherpa open a climbing school?
4. What are the Seven Summits? How do they compare?
5. What is the toughest challenge that climbers face when they climb Mount Everest? Explain.